SPICED
BLACK
Coffee

Inga Marie

ARCHWAY
PUBLISHING

Archway Publishing books may be ordered through booksellers or by contacting:

Archway Publishing
1663 Liberty Drive
Bloomington, IN 47403
www.archwaypublishing.com
844-669-3957

ISBN: 978-1-6657-3851-4 (sc)
ISBN: 978-1-6657-3852-1 (e)

Library of Congress Control Number: 2023903013

Print information available on the last page.

Archway Publishing rev. date: 03/02/2023

ABOUT THE BOOK

This book illustrates a collection of life experiences of heartbreak, pain, rejection, love, and healing. It is a collection of poems, an art of vivid emotions and the challenges of life to be shared with the reader, but with gratitude and laughter through these moments.

A SPECIAL PRAYER FOR MY READER

I pray that God will grant me the courage to be able to understand my weaknesses and work on them to change for the better. I pray also, that God will grant me patience and the ability to be calm in *all* situations … to be a better person, wife, mother, sister, daughter, and citizen, and for the ability to express without doubting myself and others, so that I can *trust*. I pray for peace in all situations and the perseverance to endure this race with joy.

Dear Reader,

It is my honor to share my poems with you through my journey of pain, tears, victory, hardships, resilience, and healing. I hope you will find solace as you read, knowing you are not alone. I also shared your pain, tears, and laughter through life's unforeseen circumstances, knowing that after the hurricane, there will be calm. I hope my words inspire you to never give up and to persevere through the hard times, as there will be joy in the end because you have a purpose, talent, and mission to share with others. This is my purpose: to share with you, my poems.

Come with me, let us travel with laughter, strength, vigor, trust, and triumph!

Your poet,
Inga Marie

ABOUT THE AUTHOR

Inga Marie is a Jamaican Canadian poet/writer who appreciates literature and poetry. It was at the age of seven years old, back in Jamaica, that Inga developed her love for poetry when she first recited a poem for a school poetry contest. Her journey of writing most of these lovely pieces began over fifteen years ago. Poetry writing is where she finds her serenity and applauds its beauty and power of healing. A survivor of domestic violence, she is an advocate for women and children against abuse. She enjoys spending time in her kitchen, cooking her favorite cuisines, and sharing knowledge from her favorite books she has read.

CONTENTS

Chapter 1
Black

Chapter 2
Long Black

Chapter 3
Espresso

Chapter 4
Affogato

Chapter 5
Cappuccino

Chapter 6
Starbucks

Chapter 7
Timmie's

Chapter 8
Blue Mountain

Chapter 9
Americano

Chapter 10
Iced

Chapter 11
Espresso Tonic

Chapter 12
Kopi Luwak

Chapter 13
Kaldi (Good Shepherd)

Chapter 14

Mocha

Chapter 15

Black-Tie

Chapter 16

Bulletproof

Chapter 17

Latte

Chapter 18

Flat White

Chapter 19
Nitro

Chapter 20
Irie

Chapter 1
BLACK

Never mock a broken man, you don't know what's in his future
or how soon his circumstances will change.

On the day I was born on this earth,
my path awaited my premeditated
footprints.
Imprinted in my mind was the
roadmap to my destination,
and the directions to getting there
sewn into my heart.

I stand amazed by the things I see,
The visions that I perceive to be.
Yet time has elapsed, and still
No signs of those things being fulfilled.
Those dreams of mine, so real and dear to my heart,
Seemed at times stuck, which tears me apart.
Seemed to be a place of no understanding,
What appeared as a sandy desert in wandering.
The fright of my fears, attempt to discourage
The dreams so real, placing them in warfare,
The same dreams that I've held on to for so long.
A fight, a war, and I must stand strong,
Never to give up or give in,
Determined to survive and win
Against all odds, I counted the cost.
Even if a battle was won, but the war is lost,
Leaving behind the frame of failure.
Encourage yourself during hard labor.
Embrace resilience and put doubters to shame.
All failures behind, and applaud my name,
Then walk by with my head looking high,
As if my head is about to touch the sky.
Smiles on my face, and I look beyond
Disappointments, focus on my dreams so grand.
The world anew as I carry my great dreams,
I could see the great journey by all means,
Dreams that are so real, which one day will be,
A reminder of the past while you enjoy ecstasy,
The reality of new joy and what will become
Victory of one hero, the grace he placed among
Others, to follow and know that they, too,
Can overcome all obstacles given to you,
Knowing that one day they will reap success.
And be blessed.

My roots are shaking,
My branches are weak and broken,
But I am still standing.
Barely straight,
I look at my seeds falling.
With a hand from my dear friend,
Twine,
I'm holding on as my new buds' sprout,
Hoping they will be stronger
To weather the storms and droughts.

A change is on its way,
I pray what comes may.
A change, I sense in the air.
A change is needed in despair.
A change in my circumstance.
Change, I need in this instance.
A change is needed immediately,
A life-changing remedy.
Change that heals broken hearts,
Change that gives a new start.
Happiness that doesn't end,
Joy that remains over and again.
Change that brings healing,
A time for restoring.
A change …

Why do you cry? Dry the tears from your eyes.
The pain is real, I know, but it doesn't have to show.
Scars from the past underline a wound that needs recast,
Journey filled with sorrow, without hope for tomorrow.
Why do you cry? Dry the tears from your eyes.
Hope and believe that there must be joy in living.
Storms of yesterday bring fruitful blossoms today.
Dry the tears from your eyes,
Stop wondering why enemies are on the front line
Awaiting your death to sign.
The loved one you desire with thoughts of burning fire
Stabs your very soul, demoralizing you.
Dry the tears from your eyes, and stop
wondering why callous hearts call from gossiping breath to maul.
Envious eyes stare,
Demonstrating cruel intent to beware.
Friends that mattered, yet they chattered.

Why do you cry? Dry the tears from your eyes.
Downfallen soul is broken by loved one's recall,
Betrayal of your character,
Brought those to laughter.
False rumor said, yet the verdict is unread.
Dry the tears from your eyes, and let me tell you why
You should dry all the tears that you've cried.
You are very special, not to mention beautiful,
Very talented—your enemies act threatened.
You are blessed, about to be a success
Intelligent, knowledgeable and of significant relevance.
Not bitter but better, an amazing personality, virtuous in character.
Why do you cry? Dry the tears from your eyes.

If I told you I was lonely, would you love me?
If I told you I was insecure and trapped in
a world of pain, would you love me?
What about my deepest darkest secrets,
including my shame, would you embrace me?
Would you take the time to see the true beauty in my
personality? Even though, at times,
I may be fragile? I must admit even at times impersonating
a child. Would you love me?

Could you allow yourself
to let my genuine core, the truest and purest part of me,
strip away the layers of my insecurities to be with me?
Would you love me?
Could you love me? The truest form
of human fidelity, yet my kindness pours out to you.
The one to pick you up when you are blue,
to tell you sweet things in your ears,
to say you can fulfill each one.
Every one of your falters and fears,
I would take them away; would you love me?

Would you love me even though I'm broke?
Yet in my heart, I would give you the entire globe.
I would take your pain and give you gain.
Would you allow me?
Allowing me would first give you pleasure,
not to mention laughter.
We may come across a bridge
that seems difficult to cross, but once
we get across, all doubts are lost.
Would you love me?

Allow me to give you the vast possibilities,
to enlighten you in your health, yet,
take care of yourself should you fall.
I would carry you across
rivers, mountains, and even other terrains.
I would never get weary should you take hold of me.
I would love you like no other
and give you all of me.
Now, would you love me?

I reflect upon your beauty and your greatness
Knowing you have placed the same greatness
inside of me.
I am your masterpiece.
How you wonderfully created me,
You've made me in your likeness.
So, I stand strong where I belong,
Conceived by your greatness,
Made in your likeness,
I love my masterpiece.

The best song of all time
Was the slow jam
We danced to
When we first met,
Even though we both
had two left feet.

I've traveled very far,
Across the oceans and seas,
To see you again,
To have you here with me.
A tormented path
to my now
serenity.

I am sorry.
Sorry for what happened today,
For all the things I did and said.
I had to tell you sorry,
Just in case
Tomorrow is not promised.

Chapter 2
LONG BLACK

It is better to be the bald eagle that finds use in a dead tree than to assume your nest is safe.

Every day I wake up, I realize that there are some things I cannot change.

I cannot change being a mother, nor would I try.

I cannot change my age, even though my face may deny it.

I cannot change the color of my skin,

cannot change my personality within.

I cannot change the color of my eyes or my height.

With good spending habits, I can change my pocket.

I cannot change my past.

Can use the negatives,

turn into positives and make them last.

I cannot change where I've been,

but I can change where I am going.

Cannot take away the scars,

but can forgive in my heart.

I cannot change the truth, even if I try to.

I cannot change yesterday,

can use those lessons for today.

When all seems to fail and you feel like things are unchangeable,

know that the Almighty One, God, is more than able.

So, when life gets difficult and you feel like you can't,

take another look and know that *yes*, you can.

You can change how to love,

and how to appreciate being alive.

A gift from above,

You can change some things today

choosing to be wiser for a better day.

You can change how and when and lead by example.
You can change the color and style of your hair
and what kind of garments you wear.
Most importantly, you can choose how to worship
and whom.
Praising the only true God
who unconditionally loves you.

A strong woman knows who she is and how she can
She knows her worth and doesn't want just any kind of a man.
Her self-worth is worth more than diamonds and pearls,
Something she was taught as a little girl.
She is not impressed by a man's cows, camels, or donkeys,
Not even those good-looking men with fine cars and houses.
A strong woman is aware of her surroundings
And works very hard for her own earnings.
She walks really proud as if to boast
Her virtue of a gift she holds dear the most.
A strong woman is not afraid to work,
Will work all day long to buy her own cloak.
She may walk miles with stacks of hay.
Selflessly, she sweats as she makes her way.
A strong woman knows that she can do anything that she wants to.
She will do the very thing that no one believed her to do.
A strong woman knows what she can and when she can.

She knows how to persevere through struggles in this land.
With persistence, she mowed her path into this powerful world,
Engaged, focused on her dreams that will unfurl.
A strong woman wakes up early,
makes her bed, even though her sheets are torn,
tattered with red.
She spreads them proudly and pretends she is rich,
Yet her richness lies in her mind and her spirit.
A strong woman washes her only drawers with her hands,
Hangs them on the line to be dried by the sun.
A strong woman knows how to use a needle.
She could sew you a designer's outfit with her spindle.
A strong woman knows her place in society
And teaches those about women's history.
A strong woman knows that she can and will become,
The symbol of life that gives wisdom.
Through her advocacy, change will come.
She holds the generation in the palm of her hands.
A strong woman knows she holds the key to carry life,
When she becomes enthroned as a great man's wife.

There's Me
This is me
Then, there's the Real Me
So, who am I?
I'm still searching
Until then, all I ask for
is your understanding.

Strong, tall,
muscular legs stood before me
Strength of horsepower,
dark and lovely
Eyes popped from my head
Got my attention
They were dark and hairy
and denotes your secret of stamina
Each leg defined, tells a story of hard work
Outlining this sexy poise as his knees jerk
Physique demonstrates pure masculinity
Depicts true pleasure in his sexuality
Hypnotized by his taunting desire
flaunting its sweet erotica,
burning with fire
Wandering eyes rolled up to the chest
Cavity buffed,
tantalizing pecs
Biceps flexed
demonstrating pure art
Grasp my breath as he captures my heart.

The first time I saw your face, I stood in wonder.

I imagined you to be someone else who didn't give a care,

as we engaged in conversation my interest of who you could be, pronged on my heart.

I could not stop thinking of the talks we would have, and my heart yearned for more.

We became friends, and then my insecurities within began to take control of me.

I wanted to love you so much and for you to do the same, but past pains and mistakes protruded, slowly whining their way in. Attempting to destroy a beautiful thing, the very essence of love that one lives for, tearing and hurting everything that the intent was to build. Two foolish hearts allowing the evil of hurt to come within the mighty walls of purity, destroying piece by piece, our souls not realizing that the core of our beings could not be touched by this madness of my insecurity. Revealing to others what was our secret and allowing the past to know our future, knowing that it could totally, demolish what we've built. Now picking up the pieces of ruins left behind, pleading with my heart and soul for a second chance given. Begging the Almighty for his forgiveness, yet deep down I'm cut to the core, bleeding on the inside, begging you for your forgiveness. To reflect on my true beauty, the radiance of love that I give to thee, uplifting thy soul and bandaging your wounds.

Preparing you for the greatness of life with me
by your side.
Smell the roses and forgive the one that truly loves you.

My Nani taught me these words
That I never used until I understood
When my friends walked away
Nani said, "Baby, don't worry, good riddance."
My first broken heart, while I cried,
She replied, "Good riddance"
When I lost my job, my Nani would say,
"That job you don't need to have,
Good riddance."
After my grandmother died,
Everything that is not good for me
I can finally stamp my Nani's approval,
"Good riddance."

This morning as I awoke, I asked myself "Why Me?"
I got up quickly, my chest pounding with anxiety,
I grieved over all my losses as no one seemed to care,
I began sobbing, looked around in despair,
I got up and moped around before dressing,
My eyes, red, all swollen from crying.
Why Me? I looked in the mirror asking,
My houses, my car, job, friends.
Wiped the tears that seemed so common,
Body filled with fatigue, and depression,
Many nights I wanted to end it all,
Contemplations in my head I recall.
The road map to life was interrupted,
By all the mishaps my mind collected.
Replayed each one daily in my head,
The wonders of life and dangers I fled.
Now this place I stand is far beyond,
The place I always had in mind.
The dreams and goals I perceived,
Now, these trials I had received.
"How do I pick up the pieces and move on?"
Portraying to the world, my bitterness is gone,
"When will I conquer the demons of my fear?"
Not questioning my failures instead, I cheer,
Telling myself that even though I've lost,
Much earthly possession I hadn't counted the cost.
I chose to see the fight instead of the battle,
Overcoming the fight first in my mind without any hassle,
Would surely give me the victory mentally,
Yet taking it into the present physically,

Disarming the dreadful voice that gave me distrust,
Making everything look ten times worse.
Now I know that what I lacked was patience,
Through hardships I had no choice, it was given,
Slowly those questions of *why*s seemed unwise,
Filling my mind with deception and lies,
Instead, I am thankful for yet another day,
I began to look forward to saying yea.
Why has "me" become "why not me"?
An overcomer, I've been given the key
To rebuild and gain even more than what I had before.
Those trials and tribulations gave me confidence.
To see the value of life in each lesson,
Now "why me" is not a question in this race.
But to get to the finish line with endurance and grace,
Keep on running until you get to the end.

Look deep into my soul,
Come closer and you will find
my love which is golden!

I hate this, I hate that
Feelings that make you say what?
Confusion, frustration, and rejection
These feelings I allowed to screw up my mission
This is not where I expected to be
You say why me, the vicious things I see
Trials and sorrows, why did this happen to me?
Nothing great, you'd say, ever comes my way
These lines repeated you'd hear yourself say
What you need is to step up your game
Stay in this race and let it speak of your name
The battles endured, lost, some won
Never to give up just keep fighting on
The invisible scars speak of endurance
Seeking answers about one's existence
Things about oneself that are disliked
Repetitious actions then asked why?
The emotions of irrationality soared
Seeking from life to offer more
The mind struggles with so many questions
Replaying in your head as they're mentioned
Waiting, anticipating for your big break
Daily decisions what impact did this make?

Hello, church sister on the seat over there
I wonder, what are you going through?
I don't know for you, but for me
I am feeling so blue
Hello, little child standing near to me
You look so happy
For you, I am glad
My life, it's filled with anger
Makes me sad.

My heart cries out from the deep
pain within
The purulent drainage that is bleeding
Hey there, can you hear me?
Do you see me?
Are you even aware of the scars inside me?

Chapter 3
ESPRESSO

It feels like I am dreaming, am I dreaming?

Life, how can I describe it to you?
The painful melodies that the wind pushes through,
Again, life how can I depict it to you? When at times tornadoes,
Whirlwinds, and hurricanes defy you
Again, I say, life, what can be said to encourage you?
When the nightmares are there swatting, beating you blue
Life passes by and by, having faith looking forward to a new day lies
Life is holding on to every breath, breathe strong, hold on
All day long,
I say to you, life don't give up when trials and tribulation seem very tough
Let me scream! Life don't give up, keep fighting the fight more than enough
Life, life, life, life is a way
A lesson to embrace the journey of your mission.

Please pray for me as I sit here in silence,
Wishing on a falling star that things would change.
Only to see that it's only a dream.
Memories of us in love, it seemed.
But now you're acting strange,
Distant is now a factor, so am I.
But you're hiding something, I know,
The truth will come out and set you free.

No more, no more of you and me,
No more, no more of what it could be.
You chose to live your life,
Continue living without me.
They say the grass is never greener,
In the long haul, you'll be the proof,
Of what could've been a good thing.

I hate my life, I even hated being a wife,
The words I would say
Repeated each day
How awful it would hurt me
How foolish, the impact I would see
Manifested before my very eye
Words used to my own demise
Words can be very deadly
They should be used wisely
Every breath, out of your mouth
Seasoned with love as they come out
Words are like building blocks
They can uplift you like a rock,
Let every word we use
Think before they abuse
Words of love and encouragement
Many words, some I mentioned
Words like "thank you" and "you're welcome"
And don't forget "please"
These words should be used with ease
And, most of all, will help you perform good deeds.

To You, I will weep,
Thy soul to keep
The pain that I feel
Is ever so real
It cuts like a knife
Suffocating my life
The words that you said
And the awful things you did
Thinking they will fade
In the bed as we lay
I guess your thoughts were wrong
Thinking I would play your song
Those strings that you pulled
Left my heart out in the cold
Soon to realize, what's in the grabs
My heart you never had
That's why this is so sad.

I never saw you coming
I was not ready when we met
Sorry, I had to shut you out.

One day it seemed I had it all
I was living the good life I recall
Drinking champagnes and giving a toast
Now I have nothing to boast
I used to tell stories to friends
Those chronicles loudly had their end
Like those fake pals that pretend
My prized possessions I had lost
Thousands of dollars exhaust
The value I placed in them
Depleted my heart and then
Placed me on the bankruptcy fence
One day I came to realize
My faith became my prize
Decided to change me
Started with my personality
I began to laugh more
Smiled ear to ear, brought the allure
My sigh to why I denied
Lost all focus on my pride
Now I am truly happy
I can honestly reply
My soul is at peace
Having belief has given me ease
Working very hard to achieve
New rewards and success accomplished
By using my abilities, ideas, and knowledge
Second chance at success is better yet
Never thought my tragic losses would be the best bet.

I sit in disbelief wondering why
you had to react and deny
Your feelings and thoughts of care
Pouring out your soul as you bare
Taking the time not to run
But standing still to understand
How messed up things really were
Denying the truth, no matter how far
The love between us has taken you to see
just how beautiful things could really be
Afraid to embrace the reality of life
Hiding behind others as life passes you by
Forgetting to consider the lessons of the past
Pressing on to prevent it from becoming full blast
Finding a little hope of light to shine through
as you express to the closest loved ones around you
Simply allowing the glare of light to take root
Then step back while the budding shoots
Watching as the circle of life spins
Revealing that love could surely win
as your legacy of courage passes on
Looked on, realizing you've already won.

Chapter 4
AFFOGATO

Life is like Letters, it must be written.

Don't argue with fools
You've just transferred
their energy to yours!

Life is like letters; it must be written
Each letter outlining mysteries of fate
Crisscross, turns, dotting the lines
Creating word by design
Each word expresses meaning
Sewn into our sense of imagining
Sensations of what it brings
Journey of life it seems
Filled with pleasure or pain
Which letter would you choose?

If I had to define regret
It would be you
You are the one person that
I should've never met
I was so young and inexperienced
Your cut was so deep
You took a piece of me with you
After all these years
I'm still in recovery.

Snowy, white pale energy forceful thrust
Presses against my heart with serene intent
Strategically, synchronized emotions unite
Kindly understanding the other's flaws
Knowing that our strength will conquer
Complimenting, connecting their souls
Kindling pureness of our divine core
Feeling the depth of your being
Eloquently stand in the purpose of will
Fulfilling each other's mission as one
Involving the Creator's spirit as three
Uniting all three and becoming one
Inviting infinity to the next life after
As love blossomed in the very end
Leaving behind seeds to carry on
Generations to come to emulate the same
Where we both will be in the next galaxy and on …

Just another day to get out of the way
Just another day what comes may
The changes of life transforming before my eyes
Dictating the essence of what alerts me to be wise
Scares me that I cannot take hold enough to control
This globe seems as it's spinning in a twirl
Tells me that my wisdom is just not enough
To stop its natural occurrences when life gets rough.

Chapter 5

CAPPUCCINO

My treasure is discovered by my thrifty friend.

People from everywhere strolled around
The venues for each product stalls
Searching for goods at bargain prices
Merchants watched in anticipation
As each passerby walked on with smirks
For the glare in their eyes tell a story within
As if they are lost and forgotten in society
As if this was their place of belonging
Array of fun displayed in the marketplace
Children, folks of old, and disabled
Strolled by anticipating handouts
Ignoring the prices set by trade
Curiosity in some of their faces
As if this was the place to entertain them
Each treasure sold belonged to another
That claimed their uselessness in their lives
Set to be sold as slaves to be captured again
Their possession of hand-me-downs from another.

Could really be a sad, darkened ending
To be thrown down once more where it was
Never to fully utilize its total effect in making a difference
The Marketplace depicts the low gloomy space of their merchants
As each buyer portrayed a mystery to their souls.

I watched in wonder, as a bird perched on the top of the tree
I looked on in amusement, and noticed its beauty in stillness
As it seeks out the forest for the perfect spot to build its nest
The straws, leaves, and branches are placed tactically to oversee
The dangers and predators of the forest as it takes a rest
This bird's imagination surpasses my curiosity as it lays eggs
As it roosts, it stays incredibly low to avoid being seen
Knowing that the dangers of the night's forest bring cruel scenes
I begin to see God's awesome creation in a different light
As the day breaks and the shadows of gray falls into the night
I appreciated the words that God's promises gave to me
To trust in every word that he spoke to thee
How much more has he provided for the grass into hay
Proficient in nutrients as the horses and cows ate and lay
He clothes the fields with colorful flowers and lilies
To fully understand without questions who he really is
Artistically flaunting these birds that fly with confident wings
Alerting through splendor, God will provide daily, everything.

Let us discuss our issues with normalcy
Pretend, please that we are a family
I would like to be the first to speak
My conversations are usually meek
Mother, I know you were broken for years
As an orphan, your heart, the trauma pierced
I hated you when I was a teen
I guess from all the things I've seen
Now I know, you did the best you could
Or
Maybe dad, you should
You should've tried harder
Instead, I had to be the fighter
When things got tough
You shouldn't have drunk so much
Now that I am grown
Let us bury the enmity you have sown
I'd hope to get things in the open
So that we can have some kind of
communication.

Please, forgive me mother
Please, I say to you father
I've blamed you both my entire life
I had to live day to day in strife
I realized that I cannot hold it against you
any longer
I knew for my sake, I had to get mentally
stronger
I'd hope to mend our relationship
Dad, my wish is, you won't pretend and skip
Mother, wipe away the tears
My intentions are to put behind these bad years
This is not about any self-blame
Or to remind you about your shame
This is merely my way to tell you
How much I've to grown to
Appreciate you
We cannot stop now
We must follow through.

I am a parent now
And this is the reason why
Father, I love you
I do not desire to say goodbye
You both are my parents,
This is my family
Let us have peace, love and unity
Guys, I am putting my entire heart in
Mom, dad, it would be a great honor
If you both join.

Chapter 6
STARBUCKS

The repertoire of the forest, harmonizes perfectly as the stage unveils the night scenes.

Relax and make your mind unwind
Listen to the musical sounds around
Can you hear the birds and the trees
As their wings and branches play
Sweet swishing with each lullaby
Do you hear the rhythm of your heart?
The melodies from each valves chant
Can you hear your breath as your lungs expand?
Each breath a whisper of air
Expressing to your mind and body
How beautiful it is to be alive
Do you hear the twinkling stars
As they play sweet sounds to each other?
Making love in harmony
Listen to the grasshoppers as they sing
Are they telling us something?
Some survival information

Or stimulating our survival instincts
Should we try to harmonize?
And even synchronize as they do?
Giving praise each day
Working together as a choir in rehearsal
Are they rehearsing to let us hear?
That they are better at love than we are?
Or merely their way of communicating
is totally in a class of its own
Their way of doing things sets them apart
As it seems that they have perfect timing
As night falls, they stand in place
And as dawn breaks, they shout in triumph.

Why are we made with tears
Intricately woven by emotions
For our own expressions
These emotions can be tamed
Like an animal
Maybe we are wild mammals
Where our emotions must soar
As the lions in the jungle roar.

Every night I cry myself to sleep
Asking the Good Lord, why me
"Why did I have to lose everything?"
As if I am losing my very being
The core of my inner soul is desperately looking for
An answer to the *when* and *why*
As if I am going to get them from the sky

"Is it true they say that you listen?"
You hear our cries, pleas, and bargains
"Will you ever come to rescue me?"
Out of the deep man-made pit
"Is my life just a dream or simply?
A reincarnation of my spirit?
Is the pain that I'm feeling really real
Or just a fabrication,
Of my wild imagination?"
Am I sleepwalking or living in reality?

But what does that mean to be real?
Am I really, real or invisible?

Walking around with dark shadows
Am I living in the now, past, or future?
How do I know that I'm not just floating
an empty vessel who got lost,
In the swing of the hustle and bustle of other living creatures?
"Am I really a human as they say,"
Or merely an animal with weird habits?"

Do I belong to the earth or somewhere else?
If I do belong here, why is it filled with so much pain?
As if all we do is live and die without any gain,
Is this how it's supposed to be?
Living day to day and expecting life as is,
"Should I fight on thinking I am here to stay,
This is where I was meant to live and die?"
But again, am I supposed to live in hell,
And wait until the day my breath expires?
If I am from this place, will I get a break,
And live joyful, singing songs of melody?

Will I ever get to ride the waves of blessings?
Singing songs of freedom from all my strife
Will the day come when I can say
I was once there in that very place?
Is there peace here on this earth?
If it is, can I get to experience it?
Or will it have to wait till I die?
To see others' joys before my very eyes.

Chapter 7
TIMMIE'S

As time dances with your journey, pause it with the strength of your footsteps.

Today I've cried the very last tears,
as they rolled down my pink-red cheeks,
I felt my heartbeat throb so hard,
it was much more than I could bear.
I began to picture myself,
and just how it used to be.
The me that I was,
the things of my past and present,
became so confusing,
Memories created in time,
as my mind began replaying the past,
then paused by the darkened climax,
challenged through each moment.
As time unwinds, racing against each second,
to impress upon this land,
my footprints of this journey.
Each second has a rhythm,
and a beat of the drums,
drumming throughout the march of life,
the good, the bad, the ups and downs.
With each prance, my feet swayed
as lazy strength moved to capture the breath
of this natural pure essence of what is called living.
I could see the reflection of my shadowing,
light glowing represented by the good old times,
happy moments then became my dark shadow.
It looked pale
as if it smelled death nearby.
My face seemed wrinkled
by the unstoppable cursed process.

Dancing had ceased,
feet weakened
by the loss of everlasting reward
due to imperfection
awaiting the destiny
of new promises
hoping that my footprints
would leave a mighty will behind
for those taking up the image to follow
what seems difficult, but not,
a great inheritance of the mission
of excellence represented by dedication,
hard work, commitment,
the faith to believe,
that one must
and can do a purpose given,
defined by the Supreme Maker,
to accomplish in this space,
therefore intercepted,
by those loved ones,
to ride the journey along,
carrying the impression of
what was a lifelong song,
now to be sung by them and their loved ones.

Blossoms bloom at the onset of summer
Sugary nectar dribble slowly
For the butterfly's dinner
Whilst branches dance in the
fragrant gentle breeze
Caterpillars humps briskly
from branches to leaves
Hangs itself in the secrecy
Of the Magnolia's twig
Carefully spindles its silky thread
Then comes the bird to pick or pluck
Yellow and black bees perched
To flaunt their stings in luck
Serenade the petals in a trance
As their wings entangled in vibration
Beautiful, amazing
Butterflies bask in the sun
Galaxies echo in laughter
Nature uttered in silence
The great transformation
Essential for all of us humans.

As I trotted along,
Riding the waves of ecstasy,
I began seeing myself growing in pride,
The feeling of might, puffed up on strife,
A sense of power,
A feeling of confidence that exalted me.
I imagined my wings and how big they would be.
Where they would lead and take me into the atmosphere
Soaring, gliding, and singing melodies of freedom.
How free it would feel,
The lack of burdens weighing on my back.
I would flap my feathers intending to flaunt
My newfound fame
I would do the jigs with my tail
In hope of the courage presented in the junction
Of the vigorous battle that I had overcome.
Displaying the art of a warrior.
Then I would jump
With the intent to touch the stars.
Looking forward to shining
brightly as the night falls away into the dawn.

Chapter 8
BLUE MOUNTAIN

Yesterday's storm will unveil your rainbow of fruitful blossoms.

For you I will do anything
I'd even bargain with the Everlasting
As I stood by your bedside
I held your hands begging you not to give up
I cried and prayed, asking God to allow his will
But at the same time pleading my case
As my manipulation I thought would work
I began to give him all kinds of promises
If he allowed you to live your life
I spoke to the nurses as they worked around the clock
I checked on your heart monitor and listened to the sound
I sat down, then I got up, impatient without your resonance
I then sat down again as if your condition would change
I began to reminisce about the *what-if*s and the *why*'s
Our loving memories seeped through my mind
Recalling the embrace, loving even the disagreements
Sometimes there were some bitter arguments
I tried desperately to wipe them away
Focus on your good old days
How you took me as one of your own

Calling me daughter; a word so momentous
A mother I considered you all along
Wiped away my tears when I thought I had no one
Always there by my side regardless
The doctor walked in, in the nick of time
To stop all the wrongs about you
He informed me about your call
And within twenty-four hours, you will leave us all

The time has come for your spirit
To go back to the Creator who made it
I started to cry once more and told him, "No"
Ran out of the room to gain self-control
How could this be, I thought
A lady who loved me would be gone
My mother is being eliminated from this world
Where would she go from here?
I found myself wandering from my fears
Where would she go to live?
I hope it is just perfect wherever that is
I could feel her spirit slipping away
I held on to her during her last breath
I held on so tight I felt her air expire.

Everything in life has a purpose
Your existence here encompasses
A time to run and a time to walk
A time to sing and a time to talk
Kicking your shoes off, strolling by the bay
Admiring the hot sun while you lay
Then dark night quickly appears
Telling a different time will premiere
Reminding once again of a time for a kiss
Getting together with loved ones reminiscing
A time to lose, a time to gain
A time to experience snowy terrain
A time to plant, a time for harvest
Mangoes, plums, apples, oranges
A time for you, a time for me
A time for blessings to receive
A time to meditate, a time to pray
Everything on earth interrelates
A time for praises and to give thanks
Forgiving those who hurt you and repent
Everything has a season, a time for us all
Living life to the fullest before the next life we fall.

The land appears dark even though the sun gleam with light
Desperately attempting to illuminate and nurture the earth
The dimness brings about a quest into the unknown
A bottomless journey into the soul searching for the profound
The unknown, it seems so hasty to hide its mysteries
Protecting and sealing its long-lasting memories
Intending to bury them in the firmament
While escaping with blustery gaseous movement
A quest that creatures pretend to replicate
As they traveled along the uncertain vales
Some stumble along the roadside injured
While others pretended, they're infallible
They galloped toward the mountains
Ignoring the warning signs as they blinked
Not realizing they had fallen off the edge
Until they wake up on the other side.

Look what she's become before her very eyes
A fallen hero whose sword is no longer used
A mother's daughter who feels like she has no one
A father's child who seeks shelter from the storm
Look at what she's become before others' eyes
Familiar faces recognized her with curiosity and wonder
Strangers see her and gaze with a puzzled glance
Once a wife who mothers her children with nature's essence
Look at her, she is torn and tattered, with wrinkled hands
Her position tells a story deep within
Of a woman who loved so deeply at a horrid cost
Now walking the streets begging for bread
She takes her place in society among the poor
And claims her fame through her talents
Knowing that one day her dreams will become
Reality of shattered to riches in a fairy tale
Like it never even happened.

As I dreamed of how it would be
Within my soul, my spirit struggles to be free
Intending for my soul to conquer my body
Creating a new image with a happy memory
My soul clings to my flesh depicting a journey
But it seemed lost amid my trials
In between its glee as it cheers my exile
The ride is rough, and I feel so trapped
Bounded by powerful forces to kidnap
I longed for this newfound freedom
Putting my tribulations in the past
Oh, I longed to feel victory that would last
As my spirit has taken over with might
I will never give up the inner fight
As the energy flickers when down
There's a beam of light that presses on
A force of gravity against mankind
Electrifying the axons of the mind
The soul, a perfect place to be
The passion of joyful, perfected in peace
A spirit so kind, it's genuine
Glows with sparkles like a diamond
A core of fresh breath deep into the heart
Given to live life as a protector or a guard
The soul is forever held immortal
Stamped with a voyage for eternal.

Forgive me of my insecurities;
Forgive me, I beg you, please
I had a mother who left me
A father who wanted to be free
A sister who was two years older
Forced to become my mother
She had to steal to give me money
So that I won't go to school hungry
Forgive me for my insecurities
Forgive me, I beg you, please
I know I can become worrisome
The truth is I'm still hurting deep down
I'm always trying to do right
By those who are against me fight
But I continue to love them
Even though hatred from them stem
One day they'll probably be my brethren
Until then I will pray for their enlightenment

So please forgive me for the way that I act
I don't always realize that I can be a jackass
Children sometimes pick up stupid behavior
Thanks to my Creator, he's my only Savior
Those things I want to shake from my past
The tears I've cried poured heavy and fast
At times I would feel like an outcast
But then I asked the Master above about me,
"Why am I here," as I fell on my knees
I begged for his understanding to see
Why his reasonings are the only key to me

I blamed myself for letting you into my being,
I blamed myself for allowing you to get close to me.
I've forgiven you for all the pain you put me through,
I forgave myself in order to be able to forgive you.
I forgive you my boss for costing me my job,
I forgive you for stealing the promotion that I never had,
I forgive you for the blessings you tried to block,
Including all the rumors you desperately were part of,
How you pause my progress from that department,
Using your hookups and networks,
Guess what it didn't work, but I forgive you.
Even the woman who gave birth to me,
Those hurtful words are constantly so disappointing,
Calling yourself my mommy,
I forgive you.
For the individual who became my ex,
The dirty tricks you played for what you expect,
I forgive you for those lies,
When you told me that you wanted me in your life,
I forgive you for using me,
For your thrills and pleasures to satisfy your desires.

For these I forgive you.
I forgive those that desperately tried to stop me,
from achieving my goals in my destiny,
No matter what you did, you did not win,
The victory was already predestined.
I've forgiven you for the bankruptcy you caused,
By all my attempts to free myself from my loss,
I forgive you, my friend, the one you never were
or became.
Your money did not impress me,
because I've forgiven you for being so imprudent,
Desperately attempting to rape my self-esteem,
Now you know what I was seeing,
For this you're forgiven.
The one I married, for better or worse,
Instead, you abused me with fistful blows,
I cried aloud and hard for your love,
What you gave instead was blows and shoves,
I thought I could make you love me,
By being there I thought you would see.

I prayed for days adding up to years,
Praying for you to stop drinking the beers,
What you gave me in the end,
Were the cheating affairs on the weekends.
You lied to give me jail time at length,
What you found was that I had supernatural strength.
I always tried to see the good instead in all situations,
Having our children cry due to your lack of emotion.
You fought in the flesh to send me back north,
In the spirit, the Almighty allowed me to stay south,
Intended to bar me from possessing the land,
Didn't you know on my head was a crown?
Put in place by the Almighty One.
Every wrong you did become my vigor,
Every tear you caused gave me power,
For this I had to learn to be better,
In order to be able to forgive you.
And I did, I've forgiven you for not having a clue,
Yes, I've forgiven you, finally, for all that you do.

You broaden my horizon, set my feet upon a plateau
The things of my life I tell you
The chains abound from the past
Secrets held behind my mask
The whippings, beatings, and bruises so many years ago
Thinking back then brings my heart sorrow
Those things have strengthened and invigorated me
Clueless to their ill-will they couldn't see
Words like "I shouldn't have you"
Deep dark hurt within felt so blue
Those words crucified the little girl's soul
Slowly divided her being as a whole
Her self-worth, confidence shattered and broken
That little girl felt all alone
Words of encouragement, love, and nurture are never done
The little girl didn't get to wear her crown
Wasn't given a chance then to become a queen
Her inner beauty shone so brightly you should've seen
You would wonder what happened to that little girl
Did she ever grow up to become a woman in this crazy world?
Forced to take her place among the elite
Wouldn't you say that was pure cruelty
A teenager without a place to dwell.

She would tell it someday very well
Feeling inadequate and lower than
At times even feeling inhuman
In a world of complication and confusion
Would she survive or fall victim?
Her inner drive to fight to survive
Must have been her only source of life
Powerful words like "long ago when"
I could've had an abortion
Told to her by the only parent
Those bondages of the burden carried so long
Lasted her some years but are now broken
She has walked into a brand-new future
Filled with wonders and adventure
She took her place among the brave
Began serving her life as if she was a maid
That little girl who never got loved
To love those who did not have
She used love to show acts of kindness
To those filled with vile and madness
Since then, this gurl has learned so much more
And married a fine gentleman whom she adores.

Today I was given the news about you
But then I sat down to think about us two
Fright filled my heart knowing
Is this decision of your life worth making?
To be that person that I ought to be
Knowing that I have another part of me
Tears rolled down my face as life begins
A new chapter of another begins to grow within
With fears, joy, and happiness of what it will take
A whole new world opened right before my face

As the days progress, nine months later
I got to see the beautiful face of my daughter
A wonderful gift I held so dear
A mother I became in a year
I held her so tight close to my heart
Looking into her eyes as we both had a new start
A mother and daughter together
A role that I will have forever
The emotions presented in bonding
The love it feels so overwhelming
I cannot fathom living without her
My life now filled with laughter.

Chapter 9

AMERICANO

Rays of faith bring hope in the breaking of dawn and joy
in the drawing of night.

Baby, baby, why do you do me this way
Baby, baby, why you had me go insane
The day you left me, I felt so broken
Now I know it was best in the end
I'm dreaming of the good times we had
Letting our dreams go was so sad
Leaving me with just a fantasy
Continuing, dreaming wishing it will be
Dreaming, dreaming of what it would be
Dreaming, dreaming of holding you in the end
Can we go back to the old days
When our love was breezy easy
Dreaming, I'm dreaming of what it would be
Dreaming, dreaming of just you and me
Can we create each other's fantasy
Starting tonight; it is quite easy
Let's get back to the old days
Creating memories of us in a daze
Dreaming, I'm dreaming of what it would be
Dreaming, daydreaming, of you and me.

I desperately tried to erase your memories
Fooling my mind that you're gone like the wind
But every time I think I've finally won
Your face shows up again haunting my soul
Like a ghost in a haunted movie played
The cruel intentions of you over and again
I told myself to let go and move on
But each time I feel liberated I dreamt of you
I cannot seem to those memories of you and I
Even though I've tried to move on with my life
I pretended to be happy—at least that's what I tell myself
False pretense it seems keeps pushing me ahead
Creating a wedge around my heart, feeling cold
Not letting any other in to know who I am
The scar inflicted was so deep, took some time to heal
Why am I so still deeply in love with you?
I know I am better without you
That's what I tell myself, but is this the truth?
When I am aware of your deception
Could I miss something that I never had?

Or the mere fact that I long to hold you
Regardless of which, the time has come
To put you and your memories behind
Now I look forward to what's coming ahead
And I hope it's not another one like you.

I looked around, all I saw
Life, living in the natural, I believe
I pinched myself. "Ouch," I said
But "look at all these problems, that won't go away
Why do we have a soul if there's no afterlife?
But if there is, "why not one of us display what it is like?"
Rose bushes in the garden, fruits, veggies, sunset to dream of
Yet poverty, food shortages, children not getting enough
Who really wonders about the purpose of the stars?
When we look around, all we hear about is war after war
Nothing is really being done by the government
Giving false promises and pretending its movement
When the truth has never been told
Generations believe in myth as they grow old
Drinking, eating, living on lies
Believing in those in authority as they secretly take lives
News broadcast propaganda, depicting humans as apes
Not deterring human trafficking as babies are raped
What comes to one's mind when Africa is referenced?
Not to mention Venezuela, Brazil predicted
Media banking on their raw ugliness
Zooms in on its starvation and the street filthiness
They fail to emphasize its beauty
Instead, they fixate on an increase in crime and poverty

"Third World Country" a name given
Where you live now could change this moment
Yet other places are hiding their shame
Boost up live TV shows, mocking fame
And trying to control when to call on God's name
The "Our Father" prayer taken out of schools
Our babies calling parents and teachers fools
Racial hatred still profiling
Hidden deeply in politicians' fake smiling
The justice system filled with injustice
A system with so much hypocrisy
Criminals paying judges off in dimes
Even going as far as favoring sex for no time
Military training youngsters seventeen, eighteen, to kill
As, though, they are too young to even have a drink
Check the quota on black men behind bars
It hurts their mamas, wives, and even lovers
Children raised without dads; boys made to become men
Taking care of their families by selling dope and using guns
Young girls looking at grown men as their fathers
Searching for acceptance and love in immoral behavior
Teen pregnancies out of proportion
Suicides, rapes, divorce, not to mention extortion

People climbing the corporate ladder based on elegance
Those getting fired just because they can
Cable TV, cell phones price scam
Stereotyping new citizens just say immigrants
Politicians stating "come forward" means deportation
Even after they have given birth to young Uncle Sam
The law doesn't protect the innocent
until proven guilty—it's guilty until proven innocent
Giving record to those considered less than
Security is insecurity
Protecting the drugs on the street
Cracks, cocaine, and heroin on increase
Given to our men, women, and even young kids
This created an epidemic in the ritzy suburban areas
Addiction on the rise, mental illness a sign
Turning a blind eye as they sell more wine
That power corrupts, money and greediness
A revelation of evil and a total mess
One taught to self-hate because of their race
A false sense of reality yet discriminates
Against the color of your skin and the features on your face
Yet ranking commoners on their country and accent
You asked, why did you leave your country?
Never considering it's a blessing to have me

You say leave, but if I do,
you'd stamp abandonment
My husband, job, and my children
Listen up, listen to what's going on
Stop being brainwashed, ladies and gentlemen
Not everyone knows when the truth is exposed
Some choose not to believe they'd rather weep
than discuss the change we can achieve
Having a boss that sleeps with the cook
Knowing if you'd say something you be given the book
Hell, no matter she's just a cheap ole hook
Going to work, not knowing if it's your last
Skating on eggshells with your trifling boss
All hell breaks loose even after trying
Hope to live through faith believing
Keeping all dreams alive in knowing
A better day, a better way,
A better tomorrow
Holding on to sanity without wallowing in sorrow
You thrive on keeping the fight
Fighting the battle with all your might
Eliminate those friends that aren't genuine
Wrong advice from mastermind regime
You know what to do,
Stop the Crap
Get on with business, call it a wrap

Pass on your knowledge and wisdom
Change lives from your experience and some
Watch seed planted sprout from the ground
Giving life new meaning to love one's profound
Allow distasteful rumors to slide off your back
Showing deadbeat people what they truly lack
Keep the dignity and faith alive
Knowing eventually, you will survive
I must say to you, though
Listen as I tell you about life, friends, and foe
Corporations banking on nepotism
Giving in disguise jobs to their families and friends
You have the education and experience
Went for the interview but the job was already taken
You work like a dog for another man
Making him rich, give him all you can
Nine to five, eleven to seven, all around
the doggone clock
When you get sick, your pay is docked
Easily replaced by another the next day
Boss plotted for this way back in May
When in April you worked and worked like a slave
Gave them overtime, the greedy sharks
Secretly they planned, and now you're all parked

Get up, be tough,
get vicious
Start your very own business
Don't be forced to take every offer
Put your all in and watch it prosper
Implement your talents, use your strengths
Focus your commitment as your investment
Don't be envious of what another man has
Focus on being better than who you were in the past
Appreciate your losses as a gift
Use it to stand strong as you uplift
Always give thanks to the Master above
Appreciate his goodness and his love
Ten years from now when you reminisce
Looking back at those times you don't miss
Putting the past behind and moving on
Moving forward with your remarkable loved ones
Some may claim, "Life is never easy to live"
Continue living without strife and forgive
Forgive those that hurt you is truly a test
It is one of the hardest things, I must confess
Your good is never good enough
Taken for granted and ready to erupt
Some drinking champagne and living it up
Wondering when you will have a breakthrough.

To find out that it starts with your mind renewed
Leave the negative and stupidity behind
As the clock ticks and running out of time
Intending to finish the race at the finish line
Imagining your days as the world turns
Rethinking your actions as the sun burns
Gaze at your babies and see
This world given, a new journey to be
Pave the way for them to follow
Give them a chance for a brighter tomorrow
Teach them the truth for what it's worth
Tell them about God, never to desert
Write a journal, document events
A hundred years from now, it was time well spent
Pass them on to the next generation
A heritage will be created by you for them
It is giving them a head start and a plan
In that journal, admit your flaws
Publicize all your mistakes and how you felt
Equip them with your skills and wisdom
If you should die; it was all said and done.

I wish you did not
have to leave
And that time
Would just stand still
Where we'd be in each
other's arms forever.

You did it again
Took me to a place of regret
I impulsively entered that
dungeon
When I had to get out of
myself
Anger boiled so hot
Temper flashed
I had to tell you to go to hell
and rot.

The earth cries for you
While the heavens rejoice at your
entrance
Stars flickered in silence
As your light extinguished its flames
below.

"Who am I, I wonder?
I drift into thought and ponder,
Just how would it be without me?
But could it be
The same
Moving from place to place?"
As a gypsy
Trying to find my identity.
"Would I be missed or just another memory"
"Another one that drifted off into the wind"
"Or do I just need to understand?"

That life is just how it stands
"But why should I take this?"
When I won't even be missed
Staying here or going there
No one seems to care
Tried it several times and failed
But I keep trying again
Trying to find where I belong
Could you be wrong?

How you've treated me
During those times we spent
Why did I get up and leave?
I torture myself asking
But the quest has just begun
Was I supposed to live without you
And you without me?
Is this how love is supposed to end?
When the sun shines on everyone
"Is it fair to say that you were so wrong about me?"
"Why did you listen to them?"
As if you do not have a mind of your own
"Who am I?"
To take this
To settle for less
Why did you pretend?
That your love was real
And this journey would be a bliss
But then you decided to jump ship
And ended up breaking my heart
Stepped on my ego a bit

And dismiss the fact that I may be that one
"It is okay, I've to say,"
But the words merely come out anyway
"Who am I to give my love to you?"
When I knew it was dangerous
Knowing love was a gamble
I've lost against the odds
But I know life still presses on
I must continue this journey
To see the world and love another
What you failed to realize
That I was strong-willed
Will continue riding up the hill
The views I will see
The experience I will have
You will die to experience them yourself
Who am I? I asked
To let you walk out of my life
And never got the chance to be your wife
"Did I jinx myself to express
My undying love for you?"
But now I am the one who's a fool

Letting someone like you be so cool
Why do we hurt others?
Are we intentional creeps
That go around lying as we leap
I say I must continue on this road
To tell others to beware
Of the dangers that they fear
Warning of you and others like the same
Letting others know way in advance
Ha-ha, you haven't won
The best of me is still here
Joke's on you thinking you're the man
When I know that you were the stupid one
As I mention, who am I
To ever let a person like you
So near, when deep in my heart I knew the cost
I must continue on this road to help others heal
As they too experience this I must tell my story
And let them know
That they're the one in total control

Today, I anxiously awaited your presence
Heard the sounds of keys as the door opens
My heart trembled knowing what your face showed
I felt my spirit fall mighty real low
I cooked and prepared dinner, what's wrong?
My love anticipated seeing you all day long
You then picked me up as a toy and threw me down
I desperately tried not to look at your face or frown
I could feel the blows to my head and face
Yet though I fear will not create a case

Your footsteps from your boots thrust my back
A reminder once more of the things you lacked
You stepped in my back as I begged
Asking you to stop as you pulled on my legs
Pleading to you for forgiveness I thought
As I peeked at your eyes, they looked distraught
Thinking my time has come for me to die
About to submerge then for a while
I said a silent prayer in my heart
Just in case it was my last
I saw my children's faces flash before my eyes
Foolish man, you cannot bring me to my demise
I kept on praying without ceasing

While my inner core kept on hoping
I still could feel the blows everywhere
I calmly pretended for you I cared
Coiled up my body in defense
Hoping you would stop at my pretense
Then I heard myself speak
As I felt myself becoming weak,
"Please don't kill me
"I am so sorry, please, please"
Give me another chance, you'll see."
You stopped as you looked into my eyes
I kept silent as I realized
That my desire to live was strong
Hoping you'll change from your wrong
Giving you yet another chance to become
A real man and not a foolish one
But the day never came to prove
The chance given mistaken for real love
Caused me bruises and a lot of emotional pain
Critiquing myself over and again
As I became older, I also got wiser
Realized that I need to teach my girls to be better
I became strong and became their strength
I was their model and teacher
I could not let the same happen to them
I had to protect them from repeating the same
At all costs I had to share my experience

Hey, ole lady, with your cart,
Filled with baggage,
City to city you depart
Hey ole man with the cane
"Tell me, what's your name?"
Tattered shoes, swollen feet
Panhandling sadly across the street

Hey, lady, tell me, what happened?
As I imagined you with so much pain
Face pressed down, staring into the ground
As you imagine moving around and around
"Hey, ole man, where is your home?"
"Do you even live in this town?"
The stories you both have to tell
The lessons of life, learned so well

"Tell me what was your vision?
Are you still interested in your mission?
Storms of life lingered so long
Slowly drenched and tuned your sweet song
Lady, those bags meticulously packed
Day to day you carry them on your back
Holes in each sac, peeking from within
Contents of life whispering their sin

"Dear, do you hold on to your fears?"
"Holding on to your past all these years?"
"Man, did you ever have children?"
"Or even a wife to love you then?"

"How about the life you've lived
Or the kind of job you had?"

"What really happened to you?"
The waves of events experienced through
Will you ever park along this journey?
Don't wait until you're on a gurney
Lady, do you dream of being a queen
Or fulfilling your fairy tales in a dream

Does your heart still flutter or gallop for anyone?
Feeling emotion for that special someone
The strength in your pain in pushing the cart
Constructed a roadblock in your heart
Your wild eyes and haunted smile
Gives your audience a predicted senile
Hey, lady, will you ever get tired?
Or wait until your breath has expired?

Memories of you flashed across the screen
What seems to be so fulfilling was only a dream
The way you held me close intending to never let me go
Wavering motion of love language telling you things
I already knew
I welcomed you with a kiss as you stood by
Afraid to feel the sting of an inevitable goodbye
The door stood wide open, but you were afraid to run
Stepped toward you to embrace the horror in anticipation
Your baby steps backward telling me that you are scared
At the same time trying to deter me to get real near
But then your arms opened wide right before my eyes
Your smile became a frown,
Your pupil began to rise,
Your voice muffled with words, you attempted to speak
Head bowed as tears began flowing down your cheeks
Your hands became limp like a dead man with a broken soul
Zombified emotions as they unfolded
As my steps got closer you disappeared
I could hear the echoes of silence that filled the air,
I stretched out my hands, inviting your fears away
Desperate measure before you go astray
Into the darkened room without any warning

My hands began to roam around in the shadow
Repeatedly, calling out your name,
While my heart pounced, singing in pain,
Pulsating every artery and vein
My fingers twitched intending to capture your presence
But the sound of the alarm ringing destroyed the essence
Waking up to my pillows, while raindrops fell
Reminding me that it was merely a dream of us all

Chapter 10
ICED

They say blood is thicker than water, be careful don't let that fool you.

Old folks would say, "You got what you bargained for"
Giving you that ultimatum was what my heart scored
Practically forcing you to take that vow
Now I am reaping the cost, wow
The things you do and say to me
When I told you how I feel
And say what's on my mind
You take off and your mistress you find
Telling and painting a picture of a witch
When your scratch needs to get itched
Your love before me was your queen
But to me you are very mean
Flowers, gifts, and material things she got
As your wife, those things you did not
My heart bled with so much anger
As my husband, you are a total stranger
The mere truth I was never loved
The other you were fond of
Poor excuses you gave as to why
I had no choice but to say goodbye.

This relationship is toxic
Love is overrated, I'm a skeptic
Nothing stays the same
Driving me insane,
This constant argument
At my wit's end
You're playing games like a boy
Now I am no longer your toy
Keep on being stupid
Your end concluded
You will come to realize
That I was incredibly wise
Now you reap what you sow
Won't be back no more
I've moved on with life
As someone else's wife
Giving him all my loving
Now you're the one lacking
Wishing for a second chance
To know events in advance
Looking back at what you had
Now I have moved on and glad.

If I had one last wish, what would it be?
The mere fact this vow is slowly killing me
I cried and prayed as hard as I could
Begging, making bargains that I may not keep
The words thrown at me infiltrated my being
Every slander took a bite out of my soul
Your selfish intentions of using me
The gem I should've been, was never
The hidden secret of infidelity discovered

The protector of my heart you should've been
Instead, you stabbed me over and over, again.

You pretended to be there for me
But hatred was all I could see
You desperately tried to tear me down,
Gestured to me with a smirk or a frown
Broken as I was, I reached out to you
Rewarded me with "Good for you, I told you so"
Even then I showed you my heart
Demonstrated with love from the start
They say blood is thicker than water
Be careful, don't let that fool you
Jealousy is a serious, secret crime
Destroys families, relationships every time
Don't be a hater just because
Love your family like it's your last
If your heart is not there to help a loved one
Don't do it and laugh behind to make fun
When someone is down on their luck
Remember it's only for a while they'll be back
Their downfall is really a success
In the long run, you'll see how they're blessed
Next time you see someone down on their face
Don't be the first to judge their case
That very situation may very well give them their break
Becoming roles models, changing lives for others' sake
Who are you to judge those that are broken
Without knowing the truth about them
They may very well be your boss
In the long haul, who really knows
Life doesn't owe us a single thing.
It could change for us in a single blink
Treat others as you'll want to be treated
Love is a circle that goes around without being depleted.

Chapter 11
ESPRESSO TONIC

It didn't hurt me, it shattered me to my core.

Never you mock a broken-down man
You do not know the plan of God's hands
Neither do you know the path to where he's going
Think twice before you start laughing and judging
Whenever you get ready to tear him down
Think about your name around town
Before you choose to drill holes in someone's heart
Use your judgment and conscious wisdom not to impart
Those troubles you love to tell others so well
Remember you could fall into those holes your darn self
Stop being so nasty with gossips about others
Start wishing greatness upon your sisters and brothers
Impress them with great inner strength of humility
And reference your kindness with love upon humanity
No one is exempted from greatness; neither are we from a fall
Stop being a snake or a snitch and be brave stand tall
Next time someone comes to you with hearsays
What are you going to say?
You start by changing the conversation

If that doesn't work, come out and tell them
Be truthful and let them know how those hurt
It hurts those you are broken the most
And why would you want to make matters for them worst
What if it was you, would you appreciate the same?
Then stop using others' names to inherit fame
Share great ideas, motivation, and encouragement
Everyone sometime or another could use them
Be a light to someone's life
Therefore, help others to survive.

I know what you felt, I see what you saw
Reliving the series of your unfaithful law
Wondering, when will this mental battle ever be won
Only to feel your inflicted pain, without anyone
Facing the truth deep within
After seeing you holding her naked sin
Emotional effect that scarred up my core
Wound so deep, scar tissue and phantom sore
Forgiving my enemies as their love affairs were told
Crushed my heart and left it in the cold
Our reckless gamble you settled for your loss
Betraying my very being, my love you exhaust
A fool telling me your love was very strong
I questioned my nights with you, and whether I belonged
Not realizing you would eventually add more pain
You tortured my heart when you left with Jane
The answer was always there, before my very eyes
After that day, I realized I am my own prize.

Hey, hey you, yes you, I'm talking to you,
The one who promised me life anew
You, who told me that you'd be there
But when I looked around, you were nowhere
Hey, you, the way you held my hand,
Telling me that you will always understand
Stared into my eyes, penetrating my soul
Pretending that you were there to console
You, who told me always and forever
Now when I call, I feel like a bother
You would pick me up when I fall
Those sweet promises I recall
Those days of telling me it's you and me
Predicting our lives, you foresee
Promises that came from the heart
Only to find that you and I are apart
Hey you, yes you, the one I truly loved
You, I'm always and forever thinking of
The journey we were supposed to be on
The broken promises that I've won
Those days of us dreaming together

The kisses we used to seal our future
But now all I see are disappointments
Like broken pieces of ornaments
You, I never stopped thinking of you
And how fulfilling it felt when it's us two
You, I hope you'll never forget
Our greatest moments unpredicted yet.

Your face, it seemed familiar except
Blurry vision eyes beheld as they wept
The contours have faded as darkness appeared
Dark, shadowy image of you seemed weird
Reflection from your pupils have rotted
Visions of us appeared stale and haunted
Can this be that memories of us have been erased?
The light was so bright back in our days
Now all I see is smoky gloom reflected from your face
Babe, this means in my life, you have no place.

Chapter 12
KOPI LUWAK

The best revenge is to become your best self.

"Will love survive the test of time
Or be conquered by the war
Of hateful crimes?"

"Is love a time machine?"
"Or will it sink like the *Titanic*
Without the captains of the ship?"
"If love survives, my curiosity asks,
Under what circumstances?"
"If love should sink without a chance
Then, what happened to the captains?"

"What did you mean when you said you loved me?"
Claiming all the wrongs you depicted to see
You picked me up and dropped me mighty low
Without expecting those negative words used gave my heart woe
My soul cried out to the Supreme Master, pleading to break
All the negative things that will not allow my soul to create
My broken, shattered, and painful past was used as an element
Of weapons thrown at me as my enemy's defense
Every ounce of story and loved ones I had told
Given to backbite me real hard you know
Trapped in them set by my enemy's hands
Reminding me that those times would never end
I cried my heart out to the one I love to understand
My true feelings of my heart to openly express and
Giving my true nature, my being to him as a gift
But it was returned to me unappreciated and unchecked
I came to realize that my love will never change someone
Or taken as a token of gem if they are truly not the one.

When you left on that indelible night
My spirit fell into the pit after that awful fight
I cried angrily and called out your name
Every word spoken; my heart maimed
Why did you leave me this way
emotionless
Opened my heart, you weren't impressed
I recall our good moments all the time
I must move on and find some peace of mind.

Dirty little one, look what you did
Someone you're not as the truth you hid
All the lies you told, pretending to be
Taunting and damaging the portrait of me
One day it will reveal the liar you are
The life you led going from bar to bar
The abuse you gave to me will be told
Your dirty little secrets will come out
Look and hear me as I shout
Get ready as I am about to tell it all
I will let the world know as I recall
The painful blows you caused me to feel
And the times you choked me on my knees
You caused this to yourself so engulf
Your abuse of selfishness was enough
As my new life has now blossomed
You must have a premonition,
That I would leave, and I
ran.

I must tell it all to help save the lives of women around the world
Telling ladies, men, boys, and girls
To respect each other without using blows
If you are angry; the fists, please resist
Use your voice and words to express
Feelings of disappointment and sadness
Don't do something you can't take back
On impulse you proved you lack
Use wisdom with knowledge to understand
No one's life is worth hurting at your hands.

To say love doesn't hurt even
When it is sweet
Is to lie to yourself
To grow together becomes
complicated
It is these trying years that
cause love to be appreciated.

The day you ignored my calls
You never considered me at all
Ignited the flame of sorrow
Not caring about us for tomorrow
Your callousness was your defense
Inflicted on me with your revenge
When I was the one that loved you
Not knowing what you would do
I trusted a baiter, one that would
Take for themselves and then
Give them another for their gain
I must consider you my lesson
Instead count it as a blessing
You will do the same again
To someone else soon
You have no conscience
Of what it takes to hurt someone
Who loved you from their core
Yet you cut me deeply, created a sore
My soul has outpoured some bleeding
Will take a long time for the healing
Deep in my heart I already know
That eventually this will blow
Your mind the same way you did me
I will watch as time passes by, what will be.

I am attracted to you
Everywhere you go, you pull me in
It's all within my circle of friends
"Am I a bird without wings
Or simply trouble that I'm always
Attracting?"

Could you find me if I was lost
In a secret place of darkness
Would you search and rescue me
if I was bound in captivity
Or would you wait until it was
too late?
Would I?
The truth is, I already am.

I thought I had the perfect family
With all of this calamity
Going on inside of me
Why did you have to be a toxin
Spreading your disease of poison?
Couldn't you have left me instead?
How selfish of you what you did?
Toxic, get out of my system
I won't let you in,
Toxic, take a hike
You won't destroy my life
You're lethal to my personality
Deadly to every part of me
Passing on to me your insecurity
You're a snake with a deadly toxin
Trying to bite me with your venom.

It's morning
My moon and stars have disappeared
And so, have you
Oh my!

Do you run? Or do you stand, face them, and get screwed?

What do you do when your past comes haunting you?

Thought you buried them and had yourself a blast

But when you least expect it, look out, alas!

The emotional scar is so hard to bear

It pierces your heart like a knife, I swear

Inexperienced lovers, the things they do and say,

Base love on their theories and feelings the wrong way

Look at the lives they've led, the baggage' they've carried

Or how many demons they've attempted to bury

Thinking there's safety in letting go

without letting the whole world know

Now you're anew, and you're like "let's party"

The demons from the past show up and say, "I am back, get ready."

Then when you least expect it, skeletons from your closet started spilling

Everything you've built your trust on exposing a twist for a second

Suddenly, oops, here it comes full--blast

A reminder of your deadly; and shameful past

These demons, attempting to rewind

The past you've long ago left behind

When you think your little secrets are safely hidden

Suggestion is, stop, look, and listen

Someone will beat you to the punch

Letting your cat out of the bag for their lunch

That will not be so desirable, or tasty, after-all

Do not allow anyone to hang you should you fall

When the mistakes of life are done,
Consider it a lesson and move on
Don't spend your entire life hiding them from any-one.

Before I close my eyes at night
Your face is the last thing I see
And the first thought
I wake up to in the light.

Today death stared intensely into my being as if it knew me
I could feel the intensity of its peculiar look
Its goal was to steal my soul and throw about the book,
Poisonous mission to conquer, programmed
To destroy all life and sinful bound
Undertaking its order, cheaply paid,
Intent to cunningly have my life laid,
Ordered to throw my life into the ground
Without any chance for a second chance
My body could sense its distasteful claws
As their fingers tend to grasp my heart
Each grip attempted to tantalize my soul
Grimaced as each finger touched to unfouled
My eyes quickly glanced at its sharp black teeth
Curiosity hit, and I pressed to look farther beneath
Cheeks grimaced with fatal laughter
This senseless emotion, desperate to slaughter
Not realizing that there was some hope left within
That death was not the answer, it is from healing
Death was caught boldfaced as a liar
Then life shouted, "You're a liar, never
Never would you be my friend
I would never ever let you in
Get lost and never be found again
You are not welcome here
Therefore, for you I have no fear."

I will stand strong and carry on
To my enemy get on, be gone
I will accomplish my mission
Yes, I am alive, and my mission has begun
So today I am thankful for my strength
To keep fighting the fight at great length
Never parting with my weapon of faith
A sound protection that bears the weight

Chapter 13

KALDI (GOOD SHEPHERD)

Regain your energy by giving praise and glory.

Today, I want to express my deepest and sincerest apology
Father, I messed up and I am so sorry
I am sorry for disobeying you
When that small voice told me "Not to"
I am sorry for always misusing your grace
Instead of spending time seeking your face
I am sorry for taking my own advice
Silly of me to bring myself to my own demise
Father, I am ever so sorry
I now see what your words told me
Your words filled with love
Your blessing soars over me like a dove
Yet, I still take your love for granted
Going day to day about my business
Each time I say I will now listen
The very thing I find myself sinning
Instead, I chose fake friends
Less time spent in your presence
The many nights I rushed my prayers
Spoke to you like you were a bother
My book of life, closed and thrown down
Refused to read it, and when I do, it's with a frown
Father, the way I've treated you is sad
Whenever I come to you, you're always glad
How could I be so selfish, self-seeking

When the outcome will only destroy me
Your wish is to give me everlasting life
Always there with your arms open wide
Please forgive me for being so foolish
I never want to become another Judas
Father, thank you for your love everlasting
Thank you for being a God all-knowing
Because of this, I am more than able
To repent and have a chance at your table
Thank you, Lord, for saving me
For this I bow to you on my knees
What a glorious day it will be
When I rise and am sitting at your feet.

Father, you're the alpha and the omega
The endless energy that you're made of
You're the answers to our questions why
As the heavens and its mysteries seem nigh
Infinite in all your ways and pure
Making the world and oceans allure
Father, you are the never-ending substance
I stand and wonder at your Potter's hands
You change the seasons as the world turns
While the sun, moon, and clouds dance around
Embracing the globe that you've created
Twinkling highlights through the nights awaited
Streams sail into seas becoming oceans
as the raindrops are falling
Entangled in a circle of life it seems
A new life begins each second beams.

The heavens look below
As the stars smile with a glow
Beholding the beauty of the earth
While creatures replenish with birth
Mountainous regions, green luscious trees
Sweet lullaby of whispers through the breeze
Demonstrating splendor and hurrah
Displaying elegance of the master's law
As the sun and moon accompany
The mystical numbers of galaxies
Each preserving their power
As the seconds tick by the hour
Protecting their territory
Lightning flashes with electricity
Masking the others unknown
As their territorial qualities are shown
Uniquely, working together
Discretely outweighs human measure
While their perfect timing kisses the skies
Stimulating the wild, as the marines swim by
Peeking into the future as seasons change
Viewing fall as the leaves turn orange
A small reminder that we have no control
Of the mysteries of this divine world.

I prayed and asked the good Lord why,
I felt the urge to crawl up and die.
The pain of this broken heart was surreal,
I pinched myself as if it was all a dream,
Except to wake up to find out this stuff was real.
I questioned the *when*'s and *why*'s after that I would cry.
I reminisced about you and me wishing for a second chance
    to be.
I looked up to the sky as if it would allow us to reconcile,
Only to realize that time and space would allow some change.
How much I wanted to tell you that I have gained confidence,
I look at your pictures and imagined your kisses,
How much I truly appreciate your presence.
I continued my prayer knowing eventually it will be answered.
As I grasped for faith in believing in miraculous opportunity
To once again express my stupidity and grant you, my apology.
I ended my prayer with thanksgiving,
As I lay down to go to sleep, I recalled your face with
    your peculiar laughter
And I smiled as I drifted to sleep.

Today is given to us to start anew
A dream we've had and prayed for came through
You and I against the odds commit
Our lives from this day forward, that's it
Listened to our hearts and from above
Knowing that "our God" has blessed our love
A vow we both shall say today
Words imprinted in our hearts we play
Forever and always, we will be
The rings are exchanged for others to see
Today, our love presented as a token
Expressed to each other in words spoken
Demonstration of God's ultimate love for us
The journey to experience it with you, is definitely
     a plus?

After receiving the call of great news
I was recalled with disappointment by you
I started to cry, but then I stopped
Emotions brought up high to be dropped
My failures once again reminded
My breakthrough was apprehended
I quickly regained my energy
Started praising and giving glory
The hiccups on this journey were difficult
The only way out was to get biblical
I began singing songs of worship
Faithfully I bowed, reminded of my purpose
I remembered his promise given to me
His goodness every day I see
Everything has a perfect timing
Weary from this mountain I'm climbing
Waiting for the Lord, it seemed hard to do
When all hell in life breaks loose
When I tried and tried on my own
I failed, miserable and alone

During those hard times, God was shown
His salvation, grace, and love given
My zeal for the mission was driven
Every downfall was a reward
Every fight remained a faithful steward
Danced to songs of joyful melody
Sang gracefully in harmony
Worshipped the Almighty God
For this, whatever came I was glad
Put all hope and faith in my Mighty Dad
His all-knowing, all-powerful everlasting
Forever will be the God of all living.

How great thou art
So holy that you only look at the heart
Very kind, precious and righteous
That no matter what, you just love us
Your love is truly undefined
It is beyond our comprehension
A God of our time and before
The Omnipotent that all should explore.

My child, my dearest loved one
You cried last night all night long
I know, I can feel all that you're going through
Last night when you cried, my heartfelt blue
Every tear that fell from your eyes
My hands were there wiping them dry
When your heart ached with pain
I felt every, pierce over and again
When you said "I am broken"
I replied to you "I will Mend"
All I ask is please know who I AM
I AM Jehovah, Yahweh, Elohim
I AM invisible, always by your side
Protecting you from dangers by and by
My dear child, please do not cry
When you worry, please take my hand
Let me lead you to the promised land
This promise I give to you
Remember it in sadness and feeling blue
I do not charge a price or a small fee
All I want to do is to set you free
To break all your chains of addiction
Before getting you to your destination
To accomplish your great dreams and vision
This is a small token to you, I should mention
Whenever, you see a homeless man
Give him a dollar and tell him "He can"
Offer him the opportunity to meet your friend
Passing his goodness on that has no end.
Lay your fears aside and trusting in him
Knowing he can give a brand-new beginning.

Chapter 14
MOCHA

Love is those sweet words that are said without a sound.

Your footsteps tread on their unique journey
While it unravels your own story
Gradually creating your legacy
Dictating to be written in history
Take action, start walking
In the end, you'll be dancing.

Love is a great song to dance to with your feet
Love is so tasty, so salivating it becomes sweet
Love is kind, and even blind at times
It can be so blind that you'll give every dime
Love could make you leave your parents
And cleave to the one you think has your behind
Love is patient, they say, and filled with joy
But at times it is bittersweet, boy, oh boy
Love can rip your heart out and leaves you in pain
It is an investment or gamble without any gain
Love can consume all your time
Love will occupy your entire heart and mind
And have you go insane when it goes wrong
Love is turning on the beat of your new song
Love is a journey, you all would agree
But when the journey has ended
It will leave you empty-handed
Without the broken heart, love is fun
It is a mystery, a great adventure to be on
Love is the sweet words that are said without a sound.

It is that look without a doubt that is crowned
Love is feeding that special someone soup on sick days
Caring, sharing, and patience in this phase
Love is understanding oneself of the other's weakness
Knowing when these flaws arise to take a deep breath
Love is letting go of fear
It is freedom of expressing to the one you hold dear
Love is God, through him it was created
A breathtaking essence of emotions elated
Love is a walk, a talk, a cry,
To the special someone to whom this applies
Love a great euphoric experience and feeling
Even better over the top when it brings one's healing.

If the oasis of the desert was in plain sight,
Then we wouldn't appreciate the tenacity,
tears, and death during the fight!

The good I see in all humanity
Surpasses my curiosity
And could be dangerous for me
Not being able to differentiate
The internal thoughts of everyone
Could be an unforeseen circumstance
But I still prefer to see good in those
It's a decision each of us choose
Seeing good could make you look naïve
When heartless ones make you grieve
Taking and cheating your innocence
Impute one's feeling of dissonance
I ask myself, what good does it do for me?
By dwelling on those good deeds, I believe
Hoping and praying that everyone I see
Have great intentions and good deeds.
That there's good in everyone to be found
By looking deeper than the surface to be shown.

Chapter 15
BLACK-TIE

The greatest you are the best of you in everything.

This foundation of mine is so fly
I can see the desire in your eyes
Precious, distinguished curves given
My mind, body, spirit from the heavens
At times it is consumed with desires
Salivating over you with my burning fire
The color may not be some of y'all favorite
To me it is very sacred
But who cares about what others think
It is a color of persistence and endurance
A color represented by hardship and slavery
My skin is soft with gentle sensuality
You may look at me and wonder
Why my ass goes beyond yonder
Always knew that I was different
Been through the flow, trampled some serpent
The shade of my skin is toned
Yet at times faced with rejection
My height is perfect just a little bit.

My legs are strong though
It is my asset
Just check out this foundation
Cannot help the daring flirtation
My strong thighs and sexy feet
They can dance and sway to your beat
My knowledge will lighten up your eyes
Make you realize that I am very wise
Creating an amusement for your smile
My physique embedded in my style
I can be funny and make you laugh
So funny you choked up till you cough
I love to confer daily events
I even know how to make one's heart pant
My spirit is filled with so much joy
Possess zeal of strength, my beauty to enjoy
The mighty pleasure I bring your way
When hearing the intelligent words
I say.

My eyes speaketh out loud
Revealing the depth of my soul
This foundation is mine
Is here on this earth to shine
But aging as time progresses on
While here I am sharing my song
Don't wait until when I'm gone
You get up to listen at the break of dawn.

My heart beats fast
I could hear every thump
Rushing through my veins
It was as if I'd been hit
By a tornado wind
I felt alive
It was then
I knew you were the one.

I made this vow to you today
I am now your wife as you say
I look forward to my life fulfilled
As you took my hands to your will
It feels like a dream
This handsome king crowns his queen
My heart skipped a beat as you swore to me for life
When you said those words, took me as your wife
My body trembled to your oath
Felt like I was going to choke
What a blessing such as this
This day I would never ever miss
I looked up in the sky and bowed thanks
As looked toward my handsome love bank.

Chapter 16
BULLETPROOF

The mind brings thoughts to life and reveals the heart.

Why is there a battle between my flesh and my spirit
My mind fighting against good and evil thoughts
Warfare against those that are in jealous mode
Those who called me friend but behind
They are on the enemy line
Pretending to like my style
Complimenting me but the truth is
They're complimenting themselves
Wishing the roles were reversed
The glare in their eyes reveals what is true
The deception of their true being
Identifying that they're on the opposite side
Seeking out information just to devour
My real self of who am I
The battle is bloody, And the rage is fierce
But this is in the mind
Of two individual who pretend
To like each other but in the end
Will have to fight till one win
The mind is such magic
Making things happen.

And pretending they have
And maybe making sure they do
The mind brings thoughts to life
And shows the true heart
Of someone undefined
Conquering enemies and wars
Could really be if it is so
That dreams do come true
Sound the alarm of the defeat
That the enemies are done
One man is standing
In the mind defeated all
But wake up … it's all a dream.

Chapter 17
LATTE

Struggles, create character through perseverance.

Struggles of life it seems each day
Worries that make you feel so grey
Marriage, children, work, and bills
Really could make your life a living hell
You think about tomorrow, wishing today
Wishing today will just go away
Life struggles, it seems so weird
These struggles could really bring you fear
This is what we call life struggles
The mere fact that we live in a bubble
The ups and downs, the highs and lows
The progress sometimes seems so slow
Life struggles are what faith is made of
Having hope is what gives us comfort
Especially in times of deprivation
Life struggles give us perseverance
Each struggle creates character
Strengthening your life to prosper
Struggles each day some say
Brings success I'd have it no other way.

Yesterday, it seemed like my dreams disappeared
Drifted away in fears that tortured my soul
I could hear the explosion of broken glass
Crisping and shattering into pieces
Like each thought of my dreams with you
Explosions of bursting flames touched my heart
Splintering piece by piece, torturing my flesh
Leaving a scarred memory of you behind
The very day I heard the sad news
About the vows you took with her
The promises you gave became a sore memory
The words professed to me were a lie
Truth was not what it seemed instead
Lies filled with self-motive and interest
Reversed my mind thinking back in time
Wishing things would be different between us
Regretting the stupidity of my actions
Of letting someone so cold right in.

Every night I go to bed I see your face
I held you tight, kissed your lips just in case
I wake up and realize it was all erased
You and I weren't together in the same place
My dreams depicted you and me together again
Every time I felt lonely and began
Waking up to lies, deceptions, and you gone
Reality kicked in when I found you with another
In July, then married in September
Breaking my heart and tearing me apart
Telling everyone that she was your heart
Never to care about my feelings but yours
Soon you will realize that there was more
As your life was fulfilled with pure sorrow
You will feel what I felt right down in my core
Begging and pleading for another chance.

In the end you will be defeated in your game
Crying every night saying my name.

Chapter 18
FLAT WHITE

Fear is a predator that will rob your entire dream and cripple your vision.

Hypocrite, you pretended to have my back,
Created slandering rumors you helped pack,
When deep down in your soul you were double-faced,
Dandled and meddled in my private case,
I could feel your stare as you cut through my core,
Envy has poisoned your soul and created an uproar,
Your desperation to become me through jealousy,
Tormented your presence you became messy,
Fakeness shone so brightly through your smile,
Radiation of corruption beamed through your eyes,
Intimidated by my strength and talents,
Intending to stop in your mind my present.

Friend or enemy, whatever you classify yourself,
Your sinister tongue hiding behind your secret self,
Haven't you realized that I invited you into my space?
Gave you a chance knowing it was a waste,
Wickedness has drowned your potential due to hatred,
Games played in your little mind but overrated,
Hypocrite, you know deep down who you are,
Hypocrite, behind my back you opened a scar,

Stop pretending to be my friend when you are not,
Hypocrite, I say how much I wanted you to rot,
Well, my strengths overcame your fears,
You did not break me, I am still here

Would I dare say hello to you in the next row,
Hell yeah! Hypocrite, I'm careful of you now,
You call me for my opinion just to see,
How smart or stupid those answers would be,
Rolling your eyes up and down over the phone,
As you held the receiver, you looked like a clown
Don't you know I was that and more,
That is why you are so insecure,
Your intentions were meant to break me down,
Pity you, as you take my name around town,
Hypocrite, you know I am blessed,
Having the blessings upon my chest,
While you were trying to destroy me,
I was already protected by the Almighty,
Hypocrite, how you have tried my style,
Sit down now and reflect upon this for a while,
Don't you know I possess favor grand,
You just cannot pass hatred about me on this land.

Think about your actions for a minute,
Those gossiping lies that you've committed,
Only to be reminded of their strengths
I will also mention I am favored at great lengths,
So next time you hypocrites, think, think,
Think before those you desperately try to sink.

Chapter 19
NITRO

Never focus on counting how many thorns your rose has; instead, admire its beauty and purpose.

Decision Making

What shall I do? I am so confused
Living in a land of confusion
Things are turned upside down inside my mind
I cannot seem to understand
What steps should I take?
Where do I go from here?
My world feels like complete darkness
I need some light to see my way
I cannot seem to grasp the answers
Where life will lead me
Am I in charge of making this decision?
I need to control of my mind
Quickly, unless a price will be paid
I cannot let my problems consume me
I will not be defeated in this race
I will press on with this conclusion
Of where this road will lead me
I feel like I'm tangled in a web
Trying to free myself to stand
To make a solid decision
And standing by it before

This path leads me to the valley
I must feel the freedom of myself
Released from the bondage of my mind
I must take control instantly
Unless I will get off this exit
Which will take me to a grime road
I must avoid doing this, knowing
That the freedom of my mind is lost
Wandering on this path could be dangerous
I must save my mind and let it shine
Making a decision that will lead me
Into a place of solace.

Rumor has it that now you're a mess
I knew it, payback would express
The way you did me in the past
Already has come around full blast
Didn't you know you would get
payback for your pet
You chose this path to leap
Now enjoy your pain as you reap

C'mon, you paved your way
Thinking you had it made
Now you've realized what they say
As memories of you fade
Could never do this to me again
Getting rid of you was best in the end

Life now is great, I must admit
I look back and say darn it
I was a fool to give you a chance
Knowing you had me in a trance
It's over now, there's no more
Pain in my heart has pierced through my core.

Rumor has it you have dollars now
While I was there for you when
You had nothing before
Go on with your money
Spend it all on your honey
We'll see what will happen
As it all comes to an end

Hello, dear, money comes
Money goes, look and see as it flows
The truth will reveal who is real
Knew the day would come
As rivers and streams become
The oceans of doubt will show
What you already know.

Chapter 20
IRIE

There's bigger, better, and greater so achieve the greatest attitude.

Yesterday, you were mine, it all seemed so real,
It's hard to disguise my feeling to believe.
The past is behind us, and the present unfolds,
But it was yesterday because it is now today, and,
Today, I looked around, and you were nowhere to be found,
You did not invite me into your tomorrow.
I guess it was so good between us yesterday.
Yesterday, I placed in my mind as time unwinds,
I guess, it was just yesterday.
Now it is out of your way, it was simply yesterday,
Yesterday, your face erased all the pain bore,
As we embraced each other yesterday,
The tears rolled down my face to demonstrate.
Yesterday, it was simply another day,
A day that I was in another place
It was yesterday, now it is gone,
And no doubt it is far along.
It was yesterday, simply yesterday.
I cannot clasp into my present,
It is just too much to bear them.
It was just yesterday when we said hey,
It was simply yesterday, now it is another day,
And you did not invite me into your tomorrow.

To see things anew and love continues.
Yesterday, but it was just yesterday.
The past is gone, and I cannot hold on.
The present is just floating along,
But I cannot catch yesterday.
It is now another day, tomorrow is coming.
I cannot grip yesterday.
It was just yesterday, I am not ready for today,
But it is here simply for a day.
Yet, it was just yesterday.

For you I will do anything
I would take the falling stars
For all our wishes I would place them nearby.
The past I would take away
and replace with a great presence.
I would have you place
your greatest trust in my heart
knowing that they are deeply hidden.
For you
I would take your brokenness and mend
the broken pieces,
only to mold you better
the second time around.
I would take you on a ride around
the world for you to see the
awesome beauty of nature
so that you would know you're made
from love and splendor.
I would kiss your hands
to express my undying love
that would take me through eternity, yet
it will continue
to the next life and
throughout the unknown.
Even if I went to the next galaxy.

I would carry your love there with me.
For you I will eradicate my weakness and
puff myself with strength where
I could lift you up when you are weak.
I would chip away at my flaws
so that I could get to your heart
I would stand confident knowing
I am in love with you, only you.

Raindrops, raindrops as hard as they fell,
The weight of their burdens so freely tell,
Their tears so mightily released,
As the clouds dance in the breeze,
Drop, drop, drip as they clapped,
Each drip clapped loudly as they splashed,
Lightning sparkles across the sky to unwind,
The marvelous mysteries from the divine.

I pray that you see my soul
Understand my only intent
Which is pure
In hope that your heart and arms
Will be wide open.

What if I told you I was dreaming
Of what was to become
It's in the processing
It won't take too long
Do you believe in dreams?
That vision of reality becomes something big
Sometimes the waiting becomes antagonizing
But it's all in the way you think
I am dreaming of what will be, how
Ouch, I must say how becomes what?
I just need one chance to allow
To prove that dreams are just that.

My heart cries out every night for you
My girls' faces flashed across my mind
Just in time to remind me of this mission
One, that I must tarry on this journey
Never intending to give up or give in
Reminded a voice deep within
I can see my girl's laughter and smile
Just as I was about to throw in the towel
I then looked up into the sky
And asked God just why, why, why?
Why am going through all of this?
My downfalls, sadness, and losses
Why am I crying every day?
As if each drop of tear will wipe them away
I can feel the throbbing of my heart
Fluttering, rising, like it's popping through my skin
It's as if my heart is truly bleeding
My mind's racing against each loss
Each neuron is evaluating the cost
My memory presses closer as it zooms
Bigger and bigger their faces appeared.

Those eyes and dimples filled up the room
Reminded me that they were very dear
I quickly remembered my job wasn't done
As I have so many hurdles to overcome
The dress-ups and make-ups to do
And all the wonderful places to go
I had hairs to comb, earrings to press on
All the games that we had left to play
I quickly drifted gears into a mom
As I put the sad memories, "pity me" behind
I had to become their strength
Even better, teaching them resilience and wisdom
The legacy of love, confidence, and respect
Telling my girls that better yet, they represented it.

Sexy, wild secret games
At nights, I call out your name
Feeling the heat that we both share
Reminded me that I still care
These provoking, secret games

Can you feel our yearning fire
Bring us back to the old-school desire
Stroking my body like weaving silk
Drinking me all up like sweet milk
Sexy, wild secret games
Secretly whispering your name

Feel me, touch me, make me scream
Take me to another place that I just dream
Let it last forever, so take your time
Please my body as I let myself unwind
Nasty, wild secret games
Yours and my secret shame.

Baby, baby why do you do me this way
Baby, baby, why you had me go insane
The day you left me, I felt so broken
Now I know it was best in the end

I'm dreaming of the good times we had
Letting our dreams go was so sad
Leaving me with just a fantasy
Continued dreaming, wished on
Dreaming, dreaming of what it would be
Dreaming, dreaming of holding you in the end
Can we go back to the old days
When your love was breezy easy
Dreaming, dreaming of what it would be
Dreaming, dreaming of just you and me
Can we create each other's fantasy
Starting tonight, it is quite easy
Let's go back to the old days
Creating memories of us in a daze
Dreaming, dreaming of what it would be
Dreaming, dreaming, dreaming.

Printed in the United States
by Baker & Taylor Publisher Services